AF507238

Facing the Challenges of Aging with Grace

C. P. Kumar
Reiki Healer
Roorkee - 247667, India

Copyright © 2023 C. P. Kumar

All rights reserved.

No part of this book may be reproduced or transmitted in any form or by any means, electronic or mechanical, including photocopying, recording, or by any information storage and retrieval system, without permission in writing from the author.

Disclaimer

While every effort has been made to ensure the accuracy and completeness of the content in this book, the author cannot guarantee that the information contained herein is error-free, up-to-date, or suitable for every individual circumstance.

The author shall not be held liable or responsible for any errors or omissions in the content of the book, nor for any damages, or losses that may arise from any actions taken based upon the suggestions or contents presented in the book.

Readers are advised to use their own judgment and discretion in applying the information provided in this book, and to consult with qualified professionals before taking any action based on the contents of this book. The author disclaims any and all liability or responsibility for any actions taken or not taken based on the information contained in this book.

DEDICATION

To all those who have embraced the journey of aging with courage, resilience, and grace.

This book is dedicated to the individuals who have faced the challenges of aging head-on, demonstrating unwavering strength and inspiring others with their determination. You are the embodiment of wisdom and vitality, and your stories illuminate the path for those who follow.

To the pioneers who have shattered ageist stereotypes and advocated for inclusivity, thank you for your tireless efforts in promoting a society that values and respects individuals of all ages.

To the healthcare professionals and researchers who have dedicated their careers to understanding the complexities of aging, your commitment to improving the lives of older adults is immeasurable. Your compassion and expertise have provided invaluable support and guidance.

To the caregivers and family members who have embraced the responsibility of supporting loved ones in their later years, your selflessness and unwavering care have made a profound difference. Your dedication is a testament to the power of love and compassion.

To the advocates and organizations that work tirelessly to combat social isolation and loneliness, your commitment to building strong connections and fostering a sense of belonging is truly inspiring. Your efforts have kindled the warmth of human connection in countless lives.

To the authors, researchers, and experts who have contributed their knowledge and insights to this book, thank you for your expertise and dedication to the field of gerontology. Your invaluable contributions have made this comprehensive resource possible.

Lastly, to every reader who seeks guidance and understanding in navigating the journey of aging, may this book serve as a beacon of hope, encouragement, and empowerment. May it provide you with the tools, knowledge, and inspiration to face the challenges of aging with grace, embracing the opportunities that lie within.

This book is dedicated to all those who believe that every stage of life is filled with purpose, beauty, and the potential for growth. May we all continue to age with grace and a zest for life.

With deepest gratitude,

C. P. Kumar

CONTENTS

PREFACE

In our fast-paced and ever-changing world, the process of aging can often feel overwhelming and daunting. As we journey through the later stages of life, we encounter a myriad of physical, mental, and emotional changes that can challenge our sense of identity and purpose. However, it is within these very challenges that we discover the potential for growth, resilience, and profound wisdom.

"Facing the Challenges of Aging with Grace" is a comprehensive guidebook that seeks to empower individuals on their unique path of aging. This book aims to provide invaluable insights, practical strategies, and heartfelt encouragement to help navigate the complexities of growing older with grace, resilience, and a renewed sense of purpose.

The chapters within this book are carefully curated to address the multifaceted aspects of aging. From understanding the fundamental nature of aging and challenging ageism to promoting inclusivity, each chapter delves into a crucial topic that affects the lives of individuals in their later years. Whether it is physical health, mental well-being, nutrition, or exercise, we explore the key areas that contribute to a fulfilling and meaningful life as we age.

In "Facing the Challenges of Aging with Grace," we explore the profound impact of social connections and offer guidance on overcoming social isolation and loneliness. We delve into the importance of nurturing relationships, effective communication, and conflict resolution to foster stronger connections with loved ones. Additionally, we tackle essential topics such as financial planning and retirement, caregiving, and the role of technology in embracing the digital world.

While this book acknowledges the challenges and inevitable changes that come with aging, it also highlights the immense opportunities for personal growth, self-discovery, and finding purpose. We examine the significance of spirituality, inner reflection, and embracing life transitions as avenues for personal transformation and fulfillment.

Each chapter provides a wealth of knowledge and practical advice, drawing on the expertise of professionals, researchers, and individuals who have faced the challenges of aging themselves. By presenting a holistic approach to aging, this book aims to empower readers to live a fulfilling and meaningful life, embracing the richness of their experiences and sharing their wisdom with future generations.

"Facing the Challenges of Aging with Grace" is not just a guidebook; it is a companion for those who seek inspiration, support, and encouragement as they embark on this remarkable journey of aging. May this book serve as a beacon of hope, guiding readers toward a life of purpose, resilience, and grace in the face of the challenges that come with growing older.

C. P. Kumar
Reiki Healer
Former Scientist 'G', National Institute of Hydrology
Roorkee - 247667, India
E-mail: cpkumar@yahoo.com
Web: https://www.angelfire.com/nh/cpkumar/virgo.html

Introduction

Aging is a natural process that every living being experiences. As we grow older, our bodies and minds undergo various changes, leading to unique challenges and opportunities. The journey of aging can be a complex and transformative one, often requiring us to adapt and face new realities. In this article, we will explore the different aspects of aging, the challenges it presents, and the opportunities it offers. We will also discuss the importance of facing these challenges with grace.

The Aging Process: A Natural Transformation

1. Understanding the Biological Changes

Aging brings about biological changes that affect our bodies at a cellular level. One important aspect is cellular aging, which is influenced by the shortening of telomeres, the protective caps on our chromosomes. Telomere shortening is associated with age-related health conditions and the overall aging process. Additionally, organ function gradually declines as we age, leading to changes in metabolism, hormone levels, and immune system responses.

2. Cognitive and Emotional Shifts

Aging also involves cognitive and emotional shifts. Memory and cognitive abilities may experience changes, and it's common to notice some decline in these areas as we age. However, research suggests that ongoing mental stimulation and engagement can help maintain cognitive function. Emotional well-being is another important aspect to consider, as older adults may face challenges such as managing stress, coping with life transitions, and maintaining a positive outlook.

Health Challenges in Aging

1. Physical Health Concerns

As we age, we become more susceptible to various physical health concerns. Chronic illnesses such as heart disease, diabetes, and arthritis become more prevalent. Functional decline and mobility issues may arise, making daily activities more challenging. Sensory changes, such as diminished hearing or vision, can affect overall well-being and independence.

2. Mental Health and Emotional Well-being

Mental health and emotional well-being are equally important considerations. Older adults may experience higher rates of depression and anxiety, often triggered by factors like retirement, loss of loved ones, or health issues. Social isolation and loneliness can also contribute to mental health challenges. Coping with loss and grief becomes more common as we age, as we face the passing of friends, family members, and even our own mortality.

Opportunities for Growth and Fulfillment

1. Pursuing Lifelong Learning

Aging presents opportunities for personal growth and fulfillment. Lifelong learning is an excellent way to keep the mind active and engaged. Exploring new hobbies and interests, enrolling in courses and workshops, and staying curious about the world can provide intellectual stimulation and a sense of purpose.

2. Embracing Self-Care and Well-being

Taking care of oneself becomes even more crucial as we age. Prioritizing physical health through regular exercise, a balanced diet, and proper medical care can help maintain overall well-being. Nurturing emotional well-being is equally essential, whether through practicing mindfulness, seeking therapy or counseling, or engaging in activities that bring joy and fulfillment. Cultivating social connections and maintaining meaningful relationships play a vital role in maintaining mental and emotional health.

3. Leaving a Legacy

Aging also offers an opportunity to leave a legacy. Sharing wisdom and experiences with younger generations can provide guidance and inspiration. Engaging in intergenerational activities fosters connections and understanding between different age groups. By contributing to society and making a positive impact, older adults can leave a lasting legacy for future generations.

The Importance of Grace in Facing Aging Challenges

Acceptance and Adaptation

Facing the challenges of aging requires grace, which involves acceptance and adaptation. Accepting the changes that come with aging and adapting to new circumstances allow us to navigate this stage of life with resilience. Embracing the process of aging and finding ways to make the most of it can lead to a more fulfilling and meaningful journey.

Conclusion

Aging is a natural process that brings both challenges and opportunities. Understanding the biological changes, addressing health concerns, and embracing personal growth and fulfillment are essential aspects of aging gracefully. By approaching the challenges with acceptance, adaptability, and a positive mindset, we can navigate the aging process with grace and live a fulfilling life. This book "Facing the Challenges of Aging with Grace" offers valuable insights and guidance on this transformative journey, empowering individuals to embrace the opportunities and overcome the challenges of aging.

Introduction

As we journey through life, one of the most critical aspects we must consider is our financial well-being, especially when it comes to retirement. Retirement is a time when we should be able to enjoy the fruits of our labor and relax without worrying about financial constraints. However, achieving a secure and comfortable retirement requires careful financial planning and preparation. In this article, we will explore the importance of financial planning for retirement and discuss effective strategies to secure your future.

The Significance of Financial Planning

Financial planning is the process of assessing your current financial situation, setting goals, and creating a roadmap to achieve those goals. When it comes to retirement, financial planning becomes even more crucial. Here's why:

1. Longevity: With advancements in healthcare and improved quality of life, people are living longer. This means that retirement can last for several decades. Adequate financial planning ensures that you have enough funds to sustain yourself throughout this extended period.

2. Rising Cost of Living: The cost of living continues to rise, including expenses related to healthcare, housing, and daily necessities. Financial planning helps you account for

inflation and ensures that your savings can withstand these increasing costs.

3. Decreased Reliance on Government Benefits: Government pensions and benefits may not be sufficient to maintain your desired lifestyle in retirement. By engaging in financial planning, you can supplement these benefits and reduce your reliance on the government for financial support.

4. Changing Economic Landscape: Economic conditions are subject to fluctuations, and your retirement savings can be impacted by market volatility. Through proper planning, you can diversify your investments and protect your savings against market risks.

Strategies for Effective Financial Planning

1. Start Early: Time is a valuable asset when it comes to financial planning. The earlier you begin, the more time you have to save and invest, allowing your money to grow exponentially. Take advantage of compounding interest by starting to save for retirement as soon as possible.

2. Determine Your Retirement Goals: Take the time to envision your ideal retirement lifestyle. Consider factors such as where you want to live, the activities you want to pursue, and any specific goals you have in mind. Having a clear vision will help you determine how much money you need to save.

3. Assess Your Current Financial Situation: Evaluate your existing assets, including savings, investments, and retirement accounts. Calculate your net worth and analyze your income and expenses. Understanding your current

financial situation is crucial for setting realistic goals and identifying areas for improvement.

4. Create a Budget: **Develop a budget that aligns with your retirement goals. Track your expenses, prioritize your spending, and identify areas where you can cut back to save more. A well-structured budget will help you stay on track and maximize your savings potential.**

5. Save Consistently: **Establish a disciplined savings habit by setting aside a portion of your income each month. Consider contributing to retirement accounts such as a 401(k) (designed by the United States Congress to encourage Americans to save for retirement) or an IRA (Individual Retirement Account). Take advantage of any employer matching contributions available to you.**

6. Diversify Your Investments: **Spread your investments across various asset classes to minimize risk. A diversified portfolio can help you weather market fluctuations and generate consistent returns over the long term. Consult with a financial advisor to determine the optimal asset allocation for your retirement goals.**

7. Consider Healthcare Costs: **Healthcare expenses tend to increase as we age. Account for potential medical costs by researching health insurance options, long-term care insurance, and Medicare coverage. Having a plan in place for healthcare can protect your retirement savings from being depleted by unexpected medical bills.**

8. Continually Review and Adjust: **Regularly review your financial plan and make adjustments as needed. Life circumstances change, and your retirement goals may evolve over time. Stay informed about new investment**

opportunities and adapt your plan accordingly to ensure its continued effectiveness.

Conclusion

Financial planning is a vital aspect of preparing for a secure and comfortable retirement. By starting early, setting clear goals, and following effective strategies, you can secure your financial future and face the challenges of aging with grace. Remember, seeking professional advice from a financial planner can provide you with valuable insights and ensure that your retirement plan is tailored to your unique needs. Start today, and take control of your financial destiny to enjoy a fulfilling and worry-free retirement.

Introduction

Retirement is a significant milestone in life, signaling the end of one's professional career and the beginning of a new chapter. While the prospect of retirement can be exciting, it can also bring about challenges and uncertainties. One of the key aspects of aging gracefully is finding purpose and meaning in this new phase of life. In this article, we will explore the importance of purpose and meaning in retirement and discuss strategies to find fulfillment during this transformative period.

The Shift in Identity

Retirement often entails a fundamental shift in identity. For many individuals, their sense of self is deeply intertwined with their professional roles. When retirement arrives, there can be a sense of loss and confusion as they navigate a new landscape. It becomes essential to redefine one's identity and purpose beyond the confines of a career title.

Reflecting on Values and Interests

Retirement provides an opportunity to reflect on personal values and interests. This is the ideal time to pursue activities and hobbies that may have been put on hold due to professional commitments. Engaging in activities that align with one's passions can bring a sense of fulfillment and joy. Whether it's painting, playing a musical instrument, volunteering, or traveling, discovering and nurturing personal interests adds purpose to retirement years.

Setting Goals and Challenging Assumptions

Retirement does not mean an end to setting goals and working towards them. In fact, it can be a chance to pursue long-held aspirations. Setting meaningful goals helps create a sense of purpose and structure. Whether it's learning a new language, starting a small business, or getting involved in community initiatives, having goals keeps retirees motivated and engaged.

Giving Back to the Community

Retirement provides an ideal opportunity to give back to the community and make a positive impact. Volunteering for local organizations, mentoring younger generations, or supporting charitable causes can provide a sense of fulfillment and purpose. Sharing one's knowledge and experience with others not only benefits the community but also contributes to personal growth and satisfaction.

Exploring New Horizons

Retirement opens doors to new experiences and adventures. Traveling, learning about different cultures, and embracing new challenges can be incredibly fulfilling. Exploring new horizons broadens perspectives, stimulates the mind, and promotes personal growth. It's an opportunity to step outside one's comfort zone and discover hidden passions and talents.

Building and Nurturing Relationships

Retirement often allows for more time to invest in relationships with family, friends, and loved ones. Strong social connections are vital for overall well-being and can contribute significantly to a sense of purpose. Engaging in regular social activities, joining clubs or groups with shared interests, and staying connected with loved ones can enrich retirement years and provide a sense of belonging.

Lifelong Learning

Retirement is an excellent time to continue learning and expanding one's knowledge. Taking up courses, attending workshops, or pursuing academic interests keeps the mind sharp and engaged. Lifelong learning not only adds intellectual stimulation but also provides a sense of accomplishment and purpose.

Embracing Health and Wellness

To find fulfillment in retirement, taking care of one's health and well-being is paramount. Engaging in regular exercise, adopting a nutritious diet, and prioritizing self-care activities such as meditation or yoga contribute to physical and mental well-being. A healthy body and mind provide the foundation for an enjoyable and purposeful retirement.

Cultivating a Positive Mindset

A positive mindset plays a crucial role in finding fulfillment in retirement. Embracing change, maintaining optimism, and focusing on gratitude can enhance the retirement experience. It's important to recognize that retirement is a phase of life filled with opportunities for growth and self-discovery.

Conclusion

Retirement is a unique phase in life that presents opportunities for personal growth, fulfillment, and meaning. By embracing new experiences, nurturing relationships, setting goals, and staying engaged with the world, retirees can find purpose and joy in this transformative period. It's essential to approach retirement with a positive mindset, cultivate personal interests, and prioritize overall well-being. By doing so, individuals can navigate the challenges of aging with grace and discover a renewed sense of purpose and meaning in their retirement years.

Introduction

In a society that values youth and vitality, the challenges faced by older adults often go unnoticed. Ageism, a form of discrimination based on age, permeates various aspects of our lives and can have profound effects on the well-being of older individuals. To truly face the challenges of aging with grace, it is crucial to address ageism head-on and promote inclusivity. This article explores the impact of ageism, challenges stereotypes associated with aging, and discusses strategies to foster an inclusive society that values and respects individuals of all ages.

Understanding Ageism

Ageism refers to the negative attitudes, stereotypes, and discrimination faced by individuals solely based on their age, particularly towards older adults. It is deeply ingrained in our society, influencing how we perceive and treat older individuals. Ageism can manifest in various forms, including social exclusion, discriminatory practices in employment, healthcare disparities, and pervasive media portrayals that perpetuate negative stereotypes.

Challenging Stereotypes

1. The Myth of Decline: One prevalent stereotype is that older adults are inherently frail, dependent, and cognitively impaired. However, research consistently highlights the heterogeneity of aging, with many older individuals leading active, fulfilling lives. It is crucial to challenge this

stereotype and recognize the diverse capabilities and contributions of older adults.

2. Wisdom and Experience: Older adults possess a wealth of knowledge, wisdom, and life experiences accumulated over the years. Rather than dismissing their ideas or opinions, society should value and seek their input. Encouraging intergenerational collaboration can lead to richer experiences and innovative solutions to societal challenges.

3. Reinventing Retirement: Another stereotype is the notion that retirement marks the end of a productive life. However, many older individuals are eager to continue working, either by choice or necessity. By creating age-friendly workplaces and offering flexible work options, society can harness the skills and expertise of older adults while promoting their continued engagement and financial security.

Promoting Inclusivity

1. Education and Awareness: Raising awareness about ageism and its impact is a crucial step in promoting inclusivity. Educational programs can challenge ageist beliefs, promote intergenerational understanding, and foster empathy towards older adults. By incorporating ageism awareness into school curricula and community initiatives, we can lay the foundation for a more inclusive society.

2. Legislation and Policy Changes: Governments and policymakers play a vital role in combating ageism. Implementing and enforcing laws that protect the rights of older adults, such as age discrimination legislation in employment and healthcare, can help create a more equitable society. Additionally, promoting age-friendly

infrastructure and services, including accessible transportation and healthcare facilities, can enhance the quality of life for older individuals.

3. Media Representation: Media has a powerful influence on shaping societal attitudes. By portraying older adults in diverse and positive roles, media can challenge ageist stereotypes and promote inclusivity. Encouraging the inclusion of older actors, writers, and directors can lead to more authentic and nuanced portrayals of aging, fostering intergenerational understanding and appreciation.

4. Intergenerational Programs: Building connections between different age groups through intergenerational programs can break down barriers and combat ageism. Activities such as mentorship programs, community projects, and cultural exchanges create opportunities for meaningful interactions, fostering understanding and respect between generations.

Conclusion

Ageism and discrimination against older adults are pervasive issues that hinder the progress towards a truly inclusive society. Challenging stereotypes associated with aging and promoting inclusivity require concerted efforts from individuals, communities, and policymakers. By recognizing the diverse capabilities and contributions of older adults, implementing age-friendly policies, and fostering intergenerational understanding, we can create a society that values and respects individuals of all ages. Facing the challenges of aging with grace requires us to confront ageism head-on and work towards building a more equitable and inclusive future.

Introduction

Aging is a natural part of life, and with it often comes a range of age-related conditions that can impact our physical health and well-being. While these conditions may present challenges, it is possible to navigate them with grace and maintain a fulfilling and active lifestyle. In this article, we will explore some common age-related conditions and provide practical tips on how to face these challenges with resilience and maintain a healthy, balanced life.

Understanding Age-Related Conditions

As we age, our bodies undergo various changes, which can lead to the development of certain conditions. It is essential to have a basic understanding of these conditions to effectively manage and adapt to them. Some common age-related conditions include arthritis, osteoporosis, cardiovascular diseases, diabetes, and cognitive decline.

Promoting Physical Health

Maintaining physical health is crucial for managing age-related conditions and overall well-being. Regular exercise plays a significant role in keeping our bodies strong and flexible. Engaging in activities such as walking, swimming, yoga, or tai chi can improve cardiovascular health, strengthen muscles, and increase flexibility. It is important to consult with a healthcare professional before starting any new exercise regimen to ensure it is appropriate for your specific condition.

Managing Chronic Pain

Chronic pain often accompanies age-related conditions like arthritis. It is essential to find strategies to manage and alleviate pain to improve the quality of life. Some approaches may include medication, physical therapy, heat or cold therapy, acupuncture, or massage. Additionally, practicing relaxation techniques such as deep breathing, meditation, or mindfulness can help reduce stress and promote pain management.

Nutritional Considerations

Proper nutrition is vital for maintaining physical health and managing age-related conditions. A balanced diet rich in fruits, vegetables, whole grains, lean proteins, and healthy fats provides essential nutrients for overall well-being. It is important to work with a registered dietitian or nutritionist to develop a personalized meal plan that takes into account specific dietary needs and any medical conditions.

Preventing Falls and Promoting Safety

Falls are a common concern for older adults and can have severe consequences. Taking proactive measures to prevent falls is crucial. This can include keeping the home environment free from hazards, installing grab bars in bathrooms, using assistive devices like canes or walkers if necessary, and ensuring proper lighting throughout the house. Regular eye exams and maintaining good vision are also essential to prevent falls.

Cognitive Health

Maintaining cognitive health is an important aspect of aging gracefully. Engaging in mentally stimulating activities such as puzzles, reading, learning new skills, or participating in social activities can help keep the mind sharp and reduce the risk of cognitive decline. It is also important to prioritize quality sleep, as it plays a vital role in cognitive function and overall well-being.

Seeking Support and Connection

Facing age-related conditions can be emotionally challenging, and it is important to seek support and stay connected with loved ones. Joining support groups or engaging in social activities can provide a sense of belonging and reduce feelings of isolation. Open communication with healthcare professionals, family members, and friends can help in navigating the challenges and finding appropriate resources.

Conclusion

As we age, it is natural to encounter age-related conditions that can impact our physical health and well-being. However, by understanding these conditions, adopting healthy lifestyle habits, and seeking the necessary support, it is possible to navigate these challenges with grace. Remember, aging is a journey, and with the right mindset and proactive approach, we can continue to live fulfilling and vibrant lives, embracing the wisdom and experiences that come with age.

Introduction

Aging is a natural and inevitable process that brings about significant changes in various aspects of an individual's life, including physical health, mental wellbeing, and cognitive functioning. While the physical effects of aging are more apparent and commonly discussed, the impact of aging on mental health and cognitive abilities is equally important to consider. As we age, it becomes crucial to prioritize mental health and cognitive functioning to promote overall wellbeing and face the challenges of aging with grace. This article delves into the significance of mental health and cognitive functioning in old age and explores effective strategies for promoting wellbeing during this stage of life.

Understanding Mental Health in Old Age

Old age is often associated with an increased risk of mental health conditions, such as depression and anxiety. The loss of loved ones, declining physical abilities, and social isolation can contribute to feelings of loneliness, sadness, and vulnerability. It is essential to recognize the signs of mental health issues in older adults and provide appropriate support. Regular mental health check-ups, maintaining social connections, and engaging in activities that bring joy and purpose can all contribute to better mental health outcomes.

Promoting Cognitive Functioning in Old Age

Cognitive functioning refers to a person's ability to process, retain, and use information acquired through thinking, learning, and problem-solving. While cognitive decline is a normal part of the aging process, certain practices can help promote cognitive functioning and delay cognitive decline. Engaging in intellectually stimulating activities, such as reading, puzzles, and learning new skills, can help keep the brain active and enhance cognitive abilities. Additionally, regular physical exercise, a healthy diet, and adequate sleep have been linked to better cognitive function in older adults.

The Role of Social Connections

Maintaining social connections is crucial for mental health and cognitive functioning in old age. Social isolation and loneliness can have detrimental effects on overall wellbeing. Regular social interactions, whether through family, friends, or community groups, provide opportunities for engagement, emotional support, and mental stimulation. Technology can also play a significant role in connecting older adults to their loved ones and reducing feelings of loneliness.

The Importance of Emotional Wellbeing

Emotional wellbeing is closely intertwined with mental health and cognitive functioning. In old age, managing emotions becomes increasingly important as individuals face various life transitions, including retirement, the loss of loved ones, and changes in health. Cultivating emotional resilience and coping strategies can help older adults navigate these challenges with grace. Expressing emotions, seeking professional help when needed, and participating in activities that bring joy and fulfillment are all essential for maintaining emotional wellbeing.

Physical Health and Cognitive Functioning

Physical health plays a vital role in cognitive functioning, and the connection between the two should not be underestimated. Regular exercise has been shown to improve memory, attention, and cognitive flexibility in older adults. Exercise increases blood flow to the brain, promotes the growth of new neurons, and reduces the risk of chronic diseases that can negatively impact cognitive abilities. A balanced diet, rich in fruits, vegetables, and omega-3 fatty acids, is also beneficial for brain health.

Mindfulness and Cognitive Resilience

Mindfulness practices, such as meditation and deep breathing exercises, have gained significant attention for their positive effects on mental health and cognitive functioning. Mindfulness helps older adults cultivate cognitive resilience, enabling them to adapt to changing circumstances and cope with stress more effectively. By focusing on the present moment and cultivating self-awareness, mindfulness can reduce anxiety, improve attention, and enhance overall cognitive abilities.

The Role of Lifelong Learning

Continuing to learn and acquire new knowledge is an excellent way to promote cognitive functioning in old age. Lifelong learning not only keeps the mind active but also provides a sense of purpose and accomplishment. Older adults can pursue formal education, take up hobbies, learn new skills, or engage in volunteer work. The process of learning stimulates the brain and promotes the growth of new neural connections, contributing to better cognitive health.

Conclusion

Promoting mental health and cognitive functioning in old age is crucial for overall wellbeing and facing the challenges of aging with grace. By recognizing the significance of mental health, maintaining social connections, prioritizing emotional wellbeing, and taking care of physical health, older adults can enhance their cognitive abilities and lead fulfilling lives. Embracing lifelong learning, practicing mindfulness, and engaging in intellectually stimulating activities all contribute to promoting mental sharpness and cognitive resilience. It is never too late to prioritize mental health and cognitive functioning, and with the right strategies and support, older adults can navigate the aging process with grace and wellbeing.

Introduction

As we age, it becomes increasingly important to pay attention to our nutrition and adopt healthy eating habits. Proper nutrition plays a vital role in maintaining our overall health, vitality, and cognitive function. By fueling our bodies and minds with the right nutrients, we can face the challenges of aging with grace and enhance our quality of life. In this article, we will explore the significance of nutrition in healthy aging and discuss practical tips for incorporating healthy eating habits into our daily lives.

Understanding the Role of Nutrition in Healthy Aging

1. Nourishing the Body

Aging brings changes to our bodies, such as decreased muscle mass, changes in metabolism, and altered nutrient absorption. To counteract these changes and maintain optimal health, it is crucial to nourish our bodies with a balanced and nutrient-rich diet. Consuming adequate amounts of protein, vitamins, minerals, and fiber can help support muscle strength, bone density, and immune function.

2. Enhancing Cognitive Function

Cognitive decline is a common concern as we age. However, research suggests that proper nutrition can play a significant role in preserving and even enhancing cognitive function. Nutrients like omega-3 fatty acids, antioxidants, and B vitamins are particularly beneficial for brain health.

Including foods such as fatty fish, nuts, berries, leafy greens, and whole grains in our diet can provide the necessary nutrients for optimal brain function.

Tips for Healthy Eating as You Age

1. Embrace a Balanced Diet

A balanced diet is the foundation of healthy eating. It should include a variety of foods from different food groups, ensuring we get a wide range of essential nutrients. Fill your plate with fruits, vegetables, whole grains, lean proteins, and healthy fats. Aim to consume a colorful assortment of fruits and vegetables to benefit from their various nutrients and antioxidants.

2. Stay Hydrated

Staying hydrated becomes even more crucial as we age. Water plays a vital role in maintaining bodily functions, including digestion, circulation, and temperature regulation. Aim to drink at least eight glasses of water per day, and consider incorporating hydrating foods like fruits and vegetables into your diet.

3. Choose Nutrient-Dense Foods

As our calorie needs decrease with age, it becomes essential to choose nutrient-dense foods to meet our nutritional requirements. Nutrient-dense foods pack a high amount of vitamins, minerals, and other beneficial compounds in relation to their calorie content. Include foods such as leafy greens, colorful fruits and vegetables, whole grains, lean proteins, and healthy fats in your meals.

4. Focus on Fiber

Fiber is crucial for digestive health and can help prevent age-related conditions like constipation and diverticulosis. Include plenty of fiber-rich foods in your diet, such as whole grains, legumes, fruits, and vegetables. Aim for a daily intake of 25-30 grams of fiber, but gradually increase your intake to avoid digestive discomfort.

5. Limit Added Sugars and Sodium

Excessive intake of added sugars and sodium can contribute to various health issues, including heart disease, diabetes, and high blood pressure. Read food labels carefully and limit your consumption of sugary drinks, sweets, processed snacks, and high-sodium foods. Opt for natural sources of sweetness like fruits and choose low-sodium alternatives when possible.

6. Adjust Portion Sizes

With age, our metabolism tends to slow down, and our calorie needs decrease. Adjusting portion sizes accordingly can help maintain a healthy weight and prevent overeating. Listen to your body's hunger and fullness cues and opt for smaller, more frequent meals if necessary.

7. Practice Mindful Eating

Mindful eating involves paying attention to the present moment while eating, savoring the flavors and textures of each bite. Slow down, chew thoroughly, and take the time to appreciate your meals. Mindful eating can help prevent overeating, improve digestion, and enhance your overall eating experience.

Conclusion

As we navigate the challenges of aging, nutrition and healthy eating become powerful tools in maintaining our physical and mental well-being. By adopting a balanced diet, staying hydrated, choosing nutrient-dense foods, and practicing mindful eating, we can fuel our bodies and minds for optimal health and vitality. Embracing these healthy eating habits not only helps us face the challenges of aging with grace but also allows us to enjoy a higher quality of life throughout the journey. Remember, it is never too late to start prioritizing your nutrition and nourishing your body and mind.

Introduction

As we age, it becomes increasingly important to prioritize our physical well-being. Regular exercise and physical activity not only contribute to better physical health but also have numerous benefits for mental and emotional well-being. In this article, we will explore the importance of exercise and physical activity in later life and provide practical tips on how to stay active and fit as we face the challenges of aging with grace.

Understanding the Benefits of Exercise in Later Life

1. Maintaining Physical Health

Regular exercise plays a crucial role in maintaining physical health as we age. It helps to prevent and manage chronic conditions such as heart disease, diabetes, osteoporosis, and arthritis. Exercise improves cardiovascular health, strengthens muscles and bones, and enhances flexibility and balance, reducing the risk of falls and fractures.

2. Enhancing Mental Well-being

Exercise is not just beneficial for our bodies; it also has a positive impact on our mental well-being. Engaging in physical activity releases endorphins, the "feel-good" hormones that promote a sense of happiness and well-being. Exercise can also reduce symptoms of anxiety and depression, boost cognitive function, and improve sleep quality.

Tips for Staying Active and Fit in Later Life

1. Consult with Your Healthcare Provider

Before starting any exercise program, it is important to consult with your healthcare provider, especially if you have any underlying health conditions or physical limitations. They can provide guidance and recommendations based on your individual needs and abilities.

2. Choose Activities You Enjoy

Engaging in physical activities that you enjoy increases the likelihood of sticking with them in the long run. Whether it's walking, swimming, dancing, gardening, or playing a sport, find activities that bring you joy and make them a regular part of your routine.

3. Set Realistic Goals

Setting realistic goals is key to maintaining motivation and avoiding disappointment. Start with small, achievable goals and gradually increase the intensity or duration of your activities over time. Remember, every little bit counts, and even short bursts of exercise can have a positive impact on your health.

4. Mix It Up

Variety is the spice of life, and the same applies to exercise. Incorporate a mix of cardiovascular exercises, strength training, and flexibility exercises into your routine. This will help you maintain overall fitness, improve different aspects of your physical health, and prevent boredom.

5. Stay Socially Engaged

Exercise doesn't have to be a solitary activity. Joining exercise classes or fitness groups can provide a social outlet and make staying active more enjoyable. Participating in group activities also offers an opportunity to meet new people and build meaningful connections, which is important for mental and emotional well-being.

6. Listen to Your Body

As we age, our bodies may require more time for rest and recovery. Pay attention to any pain, discomfort, or excessive fatigue during or after exercise. It's essential to listen to your body's signals and make adjustments to your routine accordingly. If needed, seek advice from a healthcare professional or a qualified fitness instructor.

7. Incorporate Balance and Flexibility Exercises

Maintaining balance and flexibility is particularly important as we age. Including exercises that focus on balance, such as tai chi or yoga, can help prevent falls and improve overall stability. Stretching exercises also enhance flexibility and reduce the risk of injury.

Conclusion

Exercise and physical activity are invaluable tools for staying active and fit in later life. They contribute to better physical health, enhance mental well-being, and allow us to face the challenges of aging with grace. By incorporating regular exercise into our routines, setting realistic goals, and choosing activities we enjoy, we can improve our overall quality of life and maintain a healthy and fulfilling lifestyle as we grow older. So, let's embrace the benefits of exercise and continue to stay active throughout our lives.

Introduction

Chronic pain is a prevalent condition that affects millions of people worldwide, especially as they age. It can have a profound impact on one's physical and emotional well-being, often leading to a reduced quality of life. However, by implementing various strategies and making lifestyle changes, individuals can effectively manage chronic pain and regain control over their lives. This article explores different approaches to finding relief and improving the overall quality of life for those facing the challenges of aging with grace.

Understanding Chronic Pain

Chronic pain is characterized by persistent discomfort that lasts for an extended period, typically more than three months. It can stem from various underlying conditions such as arthritis, fibromyalgia, neuropathy, or previous injuries. It is important to acknowledge that chronic pain is a complex and multifaceted issue, requiring a holistic approach for effective management.

Seeking Professional Help

1. Consult a Healthcare Provider: If you are experiencing chronic pain, the first step is to consult a healthcare provider, such as a primary care physician or a pain specialist. They can evaluate your condition, provide an accurate diagnosis, and recommend appropriate treatment options.

2. Pain Management Techniques: Healthcare providers may suggest a combination of treatments, including medication, physical therapy, acupuncture, or chiropractic care. These techniques aim to reduce pain, improve mobility, and enhance overall well-being.

Medication and Alternative Treatments

1. Prescription Medications: Depending on the type and severity of your chronic pain, your healthcare provider may prescribe pain-relieving medications such as nonsteroidal anti-inflammatory drugs (NSAIDs), opioids, or antidepressants. It is crucial to follow your doctor's instructions and be aware of potential side effects and risks.

2. Alternative Therapies: In addition to conventional medication, alternative treatments like acupuncture, massage therapy, and herbal remedies have shown promise in alleviating chronic pain. However, it's important to consult with a qualified practitioner before trying these approaches.

Physical Activity and Exercise

1. Low-Impact Exercises: Engaging in regular physical activity can be immensely beneficial for managing chronic pain. Low-impact exercises like walking, swimming, or cycling can help strengthen muscles, increase flexibility, and release endorphins, which act as natural pain relievers.

2. Stretching and Strength Training: Incorporating stretching exercises and strength training into your routine can improve joint stability, reduce stiffness, and enhance overall physical function. However, it's essential to start slowly and gradually increase intensity to avoid exacerbating pain.

Mind-Body Techniques

1. Meditation and Relaxation: **Mindfulness meditation and deep breathing exercises can help calm the mind, reduce stress, and alleviate pain perception. Integrating relaxation techniques into daily life can enhance overall well-being and serve as a valuable coping mechanism.**

2. Cognitive-Behavioral Therapy (CBT): **CBT focuses on identifying and modifying negative thought patterns and behaviors associated with chronic pain. It helps individuals develop effective coping strategies, manage stress, and improve their emotional well-being.**

Lifestyle Modifications

1. Healthy Diet: **A balanced and nutritious diet plays a crucial role in managing chronic pain. Incorporate anti-inflammatory foods such as fruits, vegetables, whole grains, and omega-3 fatty acids while minimizing processed foods, sugars, and saturated fats.**

2. Adequate Sleep: **Getting enough restful sleep is essential for pain management and overall health. Establishing a regular sleep routine, creating a comfortable sleep environment, and practicing relaxation techniques can contribute to better sleep quality.**

3. Stress Reduction: **Chronic pain often exacerbates stress, and vice versa. Engage in activities that promote relaxation and stress reduction, such as practicing yoga, spending time in nature, pursuing hobbies, or connecting with loved ones.**

Support Systems and Self-Care

1. Support Groups: Joining support groups or seeking therapy can provide an invaluable sense of community and emotional support. Interacting with individuals facing similar challenges can offer practical advice, empathy, and encouragement.

2. Self-Care Practices: Prioritizing self-care is crucial for managing chronic pain. Engage in activities that bring joy and relaxation, such as reading, listening to music, practicing mindfulness, taking warm baths, or indulging in hobbies.

Conclusion

While chronic pain may present significant challenges, it is possible to find relief and improve one's quality of life. By adopting a multifaceted approach that includes seeking professional help, exploring medication and alternative treatments, incorporating physical activity and exercise, practicing mind-body techniques, making lifestyle modifications, and building a strong support system, individuals can regain control over their lives and face the challenges of aging with grace. Remember, everyone's journey is unique, and it may require patience and experimentation to find the combination of strategies that work best for you.

Introduction

As we journey through life, one inevitable aspect of aging is the gradual decline of our senses. Vision and hearing loss are common age-related conditions that can significantly impact our quality of life. However, by acknowledging and understanding these changes, we can adapt and navigate through them with grace. In this article, we will explore the challenges posed by age-related vision and hearing loss and discuss practical strategies for adapting and thriving in the face of these changes.

The Impact of Age-Related Vision Loss

Vision loss is a common occurrence as we age, and it can have a profound impact on our daily lives. Recognizing the signs of vision loss is crucial in addressing and managing the condition effectively. Some common signs include a gradual decline in visual acuity, increased difficulty reading or recognizing faces, and decreased sensitivity to contrast and colors.

Coping with vision loss requires proactive measures. Regular eye examinations are essential for early detection and timely intervention. Consulting with an eye care professional can help identify specific vision impairments and prescribe appropriate solutions, such as glasses, magnifiers, or contact lenses. Additionally, implementing proper lighting and contrast in living spaces can enhance visibility and reduce strain on the eyes.

Embracing new technologies and accessibility features can also make a significant difference in adapting to vision loss. Many devices and applications offer text-to-speech capabilities, large font sizes, and adjustable contrast settings. Learning to utilize these resources empowers individuals to regain independence and access information more comfortably.

The Challenges of Age-Related Hearing Loss

Hearing loss is another common age-related condition that affects many individuals. It can range from mild to severe, making communication and engagement with the world challenging. Identifying the signs of hearing loss is essential to seek appropriate support. These signs may include difficulty following conversations, frequently asking others to repeat themselves, or perceiving muffled sounds.

Addressing hearing loss often begins with a comprehensive hearing evaluation performed by an audiologist. The results of the evaluation can help determine the degree and type of hearing loss, which guides the selection of appropriate interventions. Depending on the severity, options may include hearing aids, assistive listening devices, or cochlear implants.

Strategies for Adapting to Age-Related Vision and Hearing Loss

1. Seeking emotional support: Dealing with changes in vision and hearing can be emotionally challenging. Connecting with support groups or counseling services can provide valuable guidance, empathy, and coping strategies.

2. Enhancing daily life: Adopting good eye health practices, such as maintaining a balanced diet and regular exercise, can support overall eye health and potentially slow down vision deterioration. Additionally, keeping living spaces organized and clutter-free can reduce the risk of accidents and falls.

3. Exploring assistive devices: In addition to glasses or hearing aids, there are various assistive devices available to help individuals with vision and hearing loss. These include magnifiers, large-print materials, closed-captioning, and amplified telephones. Exploring and utilizing these tools can significantly improve daily functionality.

4. Communication strategies: When engaging in conversations, using visual cues, such as facial expressions and gestures, can assist in understanding context. For individuals with hearing loss, finding quiet environments, facing the speaker directly, and asking for clarification can enhance communication effectiveness.

5. Embracing technology: Technology offers a wealth of solutions for individuals with vision and hearing loss. Voice-controlled virtual assistants, smartphone apps, and assistive listening devices can all contribute to improved accessibility and independence.

Conclusion

Age-related vision and hearing loss can present unique challenges as we grow older. However, by acknowledging and understanding these changes, we can adapt and thrive in the face of adversity. Regular eye and hearing examinations, utilization of assistive devices, adopting good health practices, and exploring technological advancements are all valuable strategies for navigating age-related vision and hearing loss. With a proactive approach and a positive mindset, we can embrace these changes with grace and continue to lead fulfilling lives.

Introduction

As we journey through life, one of the challenges we often face is the process of aging. Alongside the physical changes that come with getting older, there are also emotional and social adjustments that need to be made. One significant aspect that affects the well-being of seniors is social isolation and loneliness. In this article, we will explore the detrimental effects of social isolation on older adults and discuss practical ways to build strong connections, fostering a sense of belonging and grace in the face of the challenges of aging.

Understanding Social Isolation and Loneliness

Social isolation refers to the lack of meaningful social interactions, while loneliness is the subjective feeling of being socially disconnected. Both can have severe implications on an individual's mental and physical health, especially among the elderly. The loss of loved ones, retirement, reduced mobility, and limited social networks contribute to the heightened risk of social isolation and loneliness in older adults.

The Impact of Social Isolation and Loneliness

1. Mental Health Decline: Persistent social isolation and loneliness can lead to depression, anxiety, and cognitive decline. The absence of social stimulation and support can exacerbate existing mental health conditions or trigger new ones.

2. Physical Health Consequences: Research suggests that social isolation and loneliness increase the risk of cardiovascular diseases, weakened immune system, and even mortality. The absence of social connections affects the overall well-being and longevity of older adults.

3. Emotional Distress: Feelings of loneliness and social isolation can lead to emotional distress, low self-esteem, and a sense of purposelessness. Such emotional states can have a significant impact on a person's quality of life.

Strategies for Building Strong Connections

1. Cultivating Social Networks: Engaging in community activities, joining social clubs, or participating in volunteer work can help seniors establish new friendships and expand their social networks. Local community centers, religious organizations, and online platforms can serve as valuable resources for connecting with like-minded individuals.

2. Maintaining Family Ties: Strengthening existing bonds with family members can provide a source of support and companionship for older adults. Regular communication, planning family gatherings, and involving oneself in family activities can foster a sense of belonging and connectedness.

3. Embracing Technology: Technology can bridge the gap between seniors and their loved ones, particularly those who live far away. Learning to use social media platforms, video calling applications, and online forums can enable older adults to stay connected and engage in meaningful interactions with friends and family.

4. Seeking Support Groups: Joining support groups specifically designed for seniors can provide a safe and

understanding environment to share experiences, concerns, and insights. These groups offer emotional support, encouragement, and opportunities to learn from others who may be facing similar challenges.

5. Exploring Intergenerational Connections: Interacting with younger generations can bring a sense of joy and purpose to older adults. Participating in intergenerational programs, volunteering at schools or youth organizations, or mentoring younger individuals allows seniors to share their wisdom and experiences while establishing meaningful connections.

Overcoming Barriers

1. Transportation: Limited mobility can be a significant barrier to social engagement for older adults. Community transportation services, ride-sharing programs, or relying on family and friends can help seniors overcome transportation challenges and access social activities.

2. Ageism and Stigma: Societal attitudes towards aging can contribute to the marginalization of older adults. Promoting awareness, challenging ageism, and creating inclusive spaces can help reduce the stigma associated with aging and foster social inclusion.

3. Mental Health Support: Access to mental health services and resources tailored to older adults can be crucial in addressing the emotional impact of social isolation and loneliness. Healthcare providers, community organizations, and online platforms can provide guidance and support.

Conclusion

Facing the challenges of aging with grace requires addressing the issue of social isolation and loneliness among older adults. By understanding the detrimental effects of social isolation, individuals can take proactive steps to build strong connections and foster a sense of belonging. Whether through cultivating social networks, embracing technology, or seeking support groups, the power to combat social isolation lies within our collective efforts. Together, we can create a society that values and nurtures the well-being of older adults, ensuring that they age with grace and enjoy a fulfilling and connected life.

Introduction

In the journey of aging, one of the significant challenges individuals face is maintaining and enhancing their relationships. As we grow older, communication becomes paramount in fostering healthy connections with our loved ones. Furthermore, conflicts are inevitable in any relationship, and resolving them effectively is crucial for maintaining harmony and well-being. This article explores the importance of communication and conflict resolution in the context of aging and offers practical strategies to enhance relationships.

The Power of Communication

1. Active Listening: The Foundation of Effective Communication

Active listening is an essential component of successful communication, allowing individuals to truly understand and empathize with their partners or family members. It involves focusing on the speaker, maintaining eye contact, and giving undivided attention. By actively listening, we validate the speaker's thoughts and feelings, fostering a sense of trust and openness within the relationship.

2. Empathy: The Key to Connection

Empathy plays a vital role in maintaining strong relationships. It is the ability to understand and share the emotions of others. As we age, it becomes even more crucial to cultivate empathy to bridge generational gaps and navigate changing perspectives. By putting ourselves in the shoes of our loved ones, we can better appreciate their experiences, validate their feelings, and strengthen the bonds we share.

3. Non-Verbal Communication: The Unspoken Language

Non-verbal cues, such as body language, facial expressions, and gestures, can speak volumes in a conversation. As we age, it becomes essential to pay attention to these non-verbal cues, as they often convey emotions that words alone cannot express. Being mindful of our own non-verbal communication and attuned to those of others helps us better understand their underlying messages, fostering clearer and more meaningful interactions.

Conflict Resolution: Nurturing Harmony

1. Understanding Conflict as an Opportunity

Conflicts are a natural part of any relationship, and how we approach them can significantly impact the outcome. Rather than viewing conflicts as obstacles, we can choose to see them as opportunities for growth and deeper understanding. By reframing conflicts in this way, we can approach them with a constructive mindset, seeking resolutions that benefit both parties involved.

2. Effective Communication during Conflict

During times of conflict, effective communication becomes even more critical. It is essential to express thoughts and feelings honestly and respectfully, without resorting to aggression or defensiveness. By actively listening to the other person's perspective and acknowledging their emotions, we create an environment conducive to finding mutually satisfactory resolutions.

3. Seeking Compromise and Collaboration

In resolving conflicts, it is important to seek compromise and collaboration rather than striving for a "win-lose" outcome. By focusing on finding solutions that address the needs and concerns of both parties, we foster a sense of fairness and equality within the relationship. This approach ensures that both individuals feel heard, valued, and respected, strengthening the bond between them.

Strategies for Enhancing Relationships

1. Cultivating Openness and Vulnerability

Creating a safe space for open and honest communication is essential for nurturing relationships. This involves being vulnerable and sharing our thoughts, fears, and aspirations with our loved ones. By allowing ourselves to be vulnerable, we invite trust and authenticity into our connections, fostering a deeper level of understanding and emotional intimacy.

2. Practicing Forgiveness and Letting Go

As we age, it becomes increasingly important to practice forgiveness and let go of grudges or past resentments. Holding onto unresolved conflicts can weigh heavily on relationships, hindering growth and preventing healing. By practicing forgiveness, we free ourselves from the burden of negativity and create room for compassion and understanding.

Investing quality time in our relationships is crucial for their growth and sustenance. As we age, our priorities and schedules may change, but making a conscious effort to spend time together strengthens the bond. Engaging in shared activities, such as hobbies or outings, provides opportunities for connection, creating lasting memories and deepening the relationship.

Conclusion

In this chapter, the importance of communication and conflict resolution in enhancing relationships is emphasized. By actively listening, practicing empathy, and being mindful of non-verbal cues, we can foster effective communication. Additionally, viewing conflicts as opportunities for growth, seeking compromise, and practicing forgiveness contribute to healthy conflict resolution. By implementing these strategies, individuals can navigate the challenges of aging, nurturing and enhancing their relationships with grace.

Chapter 13. Caregiving and Long-Term Care
Balancing Independence and Support

Introduction

As we age, it becomes increasingly important to address the challenges that come with aging and ensure a graceful transition into the later stages of life. One of the key aspects of this transition is caregiving and long-term care, which involves striking a delicate balance between independence and support. In this article, we will explore the significance of caregiving, the challenges it presents, and how we can approach it to maintain dignity and quality of life for our aging loved ones.

Understanding Caregiving

1. The Role of Caregiving

Caregiving encompasses a range of responsibilities aimed at providing physical, emotional, and social support to individuals who require assistance in their day-to-day lives. Caregivers often include family members, friends, or professional caregivers, and their role is crucial in maintaining the well-being and independence of aging individuals.

2. The Importance of Independence

Preserving independence is vital for the overall well-being and self-esteem of older adults. Maintaining a sense of control and autonomy allows them to lead fulfilling lives while still receiving the necessary support. Independence should be encouraged whenever possible to foster a positive and empowering caregiving experience.

Challenges in Caregiving

1. Balancing Support and Autonomy

Finding the right balance between providing adequate support and allowing individuals to make their own decisions can be challenging. Caregivers must be mindful of their loved ones' wishes and preferences, respecting their autonomy while ensuring their safety and well-being.

2. Emotional and Physical Strain

Caregiving can be emotionally and physically demanding, leading to burnout and stress. Caregivers must prioritize self-care and seek support from others to maintain their own well-being. Additionally, it is essential to recognize and address the emotional impact on the care recipient, as they may experience feelings of guilt, loss, or frustration.

Approaching Long-Term Care

1. Open Communication

Effective communication is the foundation of a successful caregiving relationship. Honest and open dialogue allows for shared decision-making, understanding each other's needs and concerns, and finding suitable solutions. Regular family meetings can facilitate discussions about long-term care plans and address any potential challenges.

2. Personalized Care Plans

Every individual has unique needs and preferences, and their care plan should reflect this individuality. Personalized care plans should be developed in collaboration with the care recipient, taking into account their goals, preferences, and values. This person-centered approach promotes dignity, choice, and a higher quality of life.

3. Professional Support

Seeking professional assistance can greatly alleviate the burden on family caregivers and ensure comprehensive care. Geriatric care managers, healthcare professionals, and social workers can provide guidance, coordinate services, and offer valuable resources to navigate the complexities of long-term care.

Promoting Independence in Caregiving

1. Assistive Technology

Advancements in technology offer numerous tools and devices that can enhance independence and safety for older adults. From medication reminders and fall detection systems to home automation and telehealth services, these technologies can enable individuals to live more independently while providing peace of mind for caregivers.

2. Community Engagement

Encouraging social connections and engagement within the community is essential for combatting loneliness and promoting independence. Community centers, senior centers, and volunteer opportunities can provide opportunities for social interaction, learning, and personal growth.

Conclusion

Caregiving and long-term care present a delicate balance between providing necessary support and fostering independence for aging individuals. By understanding the role of caregiving, acknowledging the challenges it entails, and adopting a person-centered approach, we can ensure that our loved ones age with grace and dignity. Effective communication, personalized care plans, and access to professional support can contribute to a positive caregiving experience for both the caregiver and care recipient. Embracing technology and encouraging community engagement further promote independence, enhancing the overall well-being of our aging population. By embracing this balance between independence and support, we can navigate the challenges of aging with grace and compassion.

Introduction

Aging is an inevitable part of life, and as we grow older, we face numerous challenges that can affect our physical, mental, and emotional well-being. However, with the rapid advancement of technology, we now have access to a wide range of digital tools and resources that can significantly enhance our lives as we age. In this article, we will explore the ways in which technology can help us face the challenges of aging with grace, empowering us to lead fulfilling and independent lives.

The Digital Divide and Older Adults

The digital divide refers to the disparities in access to and usage of technology among different groups in society. Unfortunately, older adults often find themselves on the wrong side of this divide, facing barriers to adopting and utilizing technology. Many seniors may feel overwhelmed or intimidated by the rapid pace of technological advancements. However, bridging this gap is crucial to ensure that older adults can fully benefit from the digital world.

To address the digital divide, initiatives have been launched to promote digital literacy among older adults. Community centers, libraries, and senior centers offer training programs and workshops to teach older adults the basics of using computers, smartphones, and the internet. Furthermore, there is an increasing focus on inclusive design and user-friendly interfaces to make technology more accessible and intuitive for older adults.

Health and Wellness

Technology has revolutionized the healthcare industry, and older adults can reap significant benefits from these advancements. Telemedicine, for instance, enables remote consultations with healthcare professionals, eliminating the need for travel and reducing the burden on seniors with limited mobility. Telehealth services also facilitate the remote monitoring of vital signs and chronic conditions, allowing for early detection of health issues and prompt intervention.

Moreover, assistive technologies play a vital role in enhancing the daily living of older adults. Innovative devices such as wearable health trackers, smart home systems, and voice-controlled assistants promote independence and safety. These technologies can monitor activities, remind individuals to take medications, and even detect emergencies, providing peace of mind for both seniors and their families.

Cognitive Stimulation

As we age, it is essential to keep our minds sharp and engaged. Technology offers a plethora of tools and applications for cognitive stimulation. Brain training apps and games, specifically designed for older adults, can improve memory, attention, and problem-solving skills. These interactive tools provide mental challenges and exercises that promote cognitive agility and prevent cognitive decline.

Virtual reality (VR) and augmented reality (AR) technologies have also shown great promise in the field of aging. VR can create immersive experiences that stimulate the senses and transport older adults to different environments, helping with therapy, rehabilitation, and reducing feelings of isolation. AR overlays digital information onto the real world, enhancing older adults' understanding of their surroundings and fostering engagement with their environment.

Social Connection and Engagement

Maintaining social connections is crucial for emotional well-being and combating feelings of loneliness and isolation. Technology can be a powerful tool for older adults to stay connected with family and friends, even when separated by distance. Social media platforms provide a virtual space for seniors to share updates, photos, and memories, bridging the gap between generations.

Additionally, online communities and interest groups cater to a wide range of hobbies and interests. Older adults can find like-minded individuals and participate in discussions, share experiences, and expand their social circles. Video conferencing and messaging platforms enable face-to-face communication, allowing older adults to see and hear their loved ones in real-time, fostering meaningful connections.

Lifelong Learning and Personal Development

The quest for knowledge and personal growth knows no age limit. Online education platforms and courses have opened up a world of learning opportunities for older adults. Whether it's exploring new subjects, acquiring practical skills, or pursuing long-held passions, seniors can engage in lifelong learning from the comfort of their homes. Online courses provide flexibility and convenience, allowing individuals to learn at their own pace and on their own terms.

Furthermore, personal development apps can promote mental and emotional well-being. Meditation and mindfulness apps offer guided practices that reduce stress, improve sleep quality, and enhance overall mindfulness. These tools empower older adults to take control of their mental health and find inner peace and tranquility.

Conclusion

Technology has the power to transform the aging experience, enabling older adults to face the challenges of aging with grace. By bridging the digital divide, promoting health and wellness, providing cognitive stimulation, fostering social connections, and facilitating lifelong learning, technology empowers seniors to lead fulfilling, independent, and connected lives. Embracing the digital world is not just about keeping up with the times; it is about embracing the opportunities and possibilities that technology brings to enhance the aging journey.

Introduction

As we journey through life, we are bound to face various challenges, and aging is one of the most significant ones. However, with the right mindset and adaptive strategies, it is possible to face the challenges of aging with grace. In this article, we will explore the importance of maintaining independence in daily living as we age and discuss adaptive strategies that can help us maintain our autonomy and quality of life.

Understanding the Significance of Independence

Independence is a fundamental aspect of human dignity and well-being. As we age, maintaining independence becomes even more crucial. It allows us to retain control over our lives, make our own decisions, and engage in activities that bring us joy and fulfillment. Independence enables us to age gracefully, maintaining a sense of purpose and self-worth.

Physical Adaptations for Daily Living

1. Home Modifications: Adapting our living environment can significantly enhance our ability to live independently. Installing grab bars in the bathroom, ramps for easy access, and removing tripping hazards are some examples of modifications that can improve safety and mobility.

2. Assistive Devices: Utilizing assistive devices can empower us to perform daily tasks with ease. Devices such

as walking aids, reachers, and jar openers can compensate for physical limitations and enable independent living.

3. Exercise and Mobility: Engaging in regular physical exercise and mobility routines can help maintain strength, flexibility, and balance. Activities like walking, swimming, and tai chi promote overall well-being and reduce the risk of falls.

Cognitive and Emotional Adaptations

1. Mental Stimulation: Keeping the mind active is vital for maintaining cognitive abilities. Engaging in activities like reading, puzzles, learning new skills, and socializing can improve memory, concentration, and overall cognitive function.

2. Emotional Well-being: Aging often comes with emotional challenges such as loss of loved ones and changes in social dynamics. Nurturing emotional well-being through activities like meditation, therapy, and maintaining social connections is essential for maintaining independence and overall happiness.

3. Organization and Planning: As cognitive abilities change, adapting organizational strategies becomes crucial. Using calendars, reminders, and checklists can help us stay organized and ensure that important tasks are completed.

Social Adaptations

1. Community Engagement: Staying socially connected is a key component of maintaining independence. Engaging in community activities, joining clubs or groups, and volunteering not only provide opportunities for social interaction but also offer a sense of purpose and fulfillment.

2. Technology and Communication: Embracing technology can bridge the gap between generations and facilitate communication. Learning to use smartphones, social media platforms, and video calling apps can help us stay connected with loved ones and access valuable resources.

3. Transportation: As driving abilities may change with age, finding alternative transportation options becomes essential. Utilizing public transportation, ride-sharing services, or arranging transportation through community programs can help maintain mobility and independence.

Financial Adaptations

1. Financial Planning: Being proactive in financial planning ensures a stable future. Establishing a budget, reviewing insurance policies, and seeking professional advice can help manage finances effectively and provide peace of mind.

2. Fraud Prevention: Seniors are often targeted by financial scams. Staying informed about common scams, safeguarding personal information, and seeking advice from trusted sources can protect us from fraud and financial exploitation.

Conclusion

Aging is a natural part of life, and while it brings its own set of challenges, maintaining independence is within our reach. By embracing adaptive strategies for daily living, we can continue to live life on our terms, preserving our autonomy, and facing the challenges of aging with grace. From physical adaptations and cognitive strategies to social engagement and financial planning, each aspect contributes to our overall well-being. Let us embrace these adaptive strategies, nurture our independence, and enjoy a fulfilling and dignified life as we age.

Introduction

Individuals may encounter various emotional struggles as they navigate the later stages of life. Among these challenges, loss and grief stand out as profound experiences that shape one's journey. Coping with bereavement and life transitions can be particularly challenging, but with the right understanding and support, it is possible to find healing and resilience.

Understanding Loss and Grief

Loss is an inevitable part of the human experience. Whether it's the death of a loved one, the end of a significant relationship, or the loss of one's own physical capabilities, each instance of loss triggers a process of grieving. Grief is a complex and individual response to loss, encompassing a range of emotions such as sadness, anger, guilt, and confusion.

Navigating Bereavement

When faced with the death of a loved one, the grieving process can be overwhelming. It is essential to acknowledge and allow oneself to experience the various emotions that arise. Denying or suppressing these emotions can prolong the healing process. It is crucial to create a support system and reach out to friends, family, or support groups who can provide comfort and understanding during this difficult time.

Honoring Memories

One way to cope with bereavement is by honoring the memories of the deceased. This can be done through rituals, such as creating a memory box or holding a memorial service, where friends and family can come together to celebrate the life that was lived. Reflecting on the positive aspects of the person's life and the impact they had on others can bring a sense of solace and connection.

Seeking Professional Help

Sometimes, the grieving process becomes overwhelming and may require professional assistance. Grief counselors or therapists can provide guidance and support in navigating the complex emotions associated with bereavement. They can offer coping strategies, help process unresolved feelings, and provide a safe space for individuals to express their grief without judgment.

Life Transitions

Loss and grief are not limited to the death of a loved one. Life transitions, such as retirement, a decline in physical health, or the loss of independence, can also trigger a grieving process. It is common to mourn the loss of a familiar routine, identity, or role in society. Acknowledging these feelings and seeking support are essential steps in coping with life transitions.

Building Resilience

While grief may never fully disappear, individuals can develop resilience to cope with loss and life transitions. It is important to take care of oneself physically, emotionally, and spiritually. Engaging in activities that bring joy and a sense of purpose, such as hobbies, exercise, or volunteering, can help in the healing process. Connecting with others and nurturing relationships is also crucial, as social support can provide comfort and strength during difficult times.

Embracing Change

As individuals face the challenges of aging, it is important to embrace change and adapt to new circumstances. This may involve letting go of past roles and expectations and finding new sources of fulfillment and meaning. Developing a positive mindset and cultivating gratitude for the present can help in navigating life's transitions with grace and resilience.

Conclusion

Loss and grief are an inevitable part of life, particularly as we age and face significant transitions. Coping with bereavement and life transitions requires understanding, support, and self-compassion. By acknowledging and processing the emotions associated with loss, seeking support from others, and embracing change, individuals can find healing, resilience, and ultimately face the challenges of aging with grace. Remember, it is through the journey of loss and grief that we have the opportunity to grow, evolve, and discover new depths of strength within ourselves.

Introduction

Aging is an inevitable part of life, and as we grow older, we face various physical, emotional, and social challenges. However, amidst these challenges, spirituality can play a crucial role in nurturing the inner self and promoting a sense of peace, purpose, and fulfillment. In this article, we explore the profound connection between spirituality and aging and delve into the ways in which individuals can embrace their spiritual journey to enhance their overall well-being.

Recognizing the Essence of Spirituality

At its core, spirituality is the search for meaning and purpose in life, beyond the physical realm. It involves connecting with something greater than oneself, be it a higher power, nature, or the collective consciousness. As individuals age, they often grapple with existential questions and ponder the deeper aspects of their existence. By recognizing the essence of spirituality, one can embark on a transformative journey that transcends the limitations of age and physical decline.

Embracing Transcendence and Finding Purpose

One of the fundamental aspects of spirituality is the notion of transcendence. It is the ability to rise above the challenges of aging and tap into a higher level of consciousness. Through meditation, prayer, or engaging in meaningful activities, individuals can transcend the limitations of the physical body and connect with their inner selves. This connection helps in finding a renewed sense of purpose and meaning, which contributes to overall well-being.

Cultivating Mindfulness and Gratitude

As we age, it becomes increasingly important to cultivate mindfulness and gratitude. Mindfulness involves being fully present in the moment, accepting it without judgment. By practicing mindfulness, individuals can develop a deeper awareness of their thoughts, emotions, and physical sensations, allowing them to navigate the aging process with greater clarity and peace. Gratitude, on the other hand, fosters a positive outlook by appreciating the simple joys and blessings of life, even amidst challenges.

Seeking Wisdom and Self-Reflection

Aging brings with it a wealth of experiences and accumulated wisdom. Spirituality encourages individuals to engage in self-reflection and introspection, utilizing these experiences to gain insights into themselves and the world around them. By embracing self-reflection, individuals can identify their strengths, reconcile with past regrets or mistakes, and cultivate a sense of self-acceptance. This process of seeking wisdom and self-reflection enhances personal growth and contributes to a more fulfilling life.

Connecting with Community and Offering Service

Spirituality is not solely an individualistic pursuit; it also involves connecting with others and fostering a sense of community. Aging individuals can find solace and support by engaging with like-minded individuals who share their spiritual beliefs and values. Moreover, offering service to others, whether through volunteering or acts of kindness, not only benefits the recipients but also deepens one's own sense of purpose and connection to humanity.

Nurturing Hope and Resilience

The aging process can be accompanied by various challenges, such as health issues, loss of loved ones, and changes in social roles. In such times, spirituality can provide a source of hope and resilience. Believing in something greater than oneself and having faith in the journey ahead can help individuals navigate through difficult times with strength and courage. Spirituality serves as a guiding light, reminding individuals that there is meaning and purpose even in the face of adversity.

Conclusion

Spirituality emerges as a vital aspect of the aging process. By nurturing the inner self through transcendence, mindfulness, self-reflection, community, and service, individuals can find solace, purpose, and fulfillment in their later years. Embracing spirituality allows one to age with grace, wisdom, and resilience, fostering a deep connection with the self, others, and the larger universe. Ultimately, spirituality offers a profound pathway to navigating the challenges of aging and embracing the fullness of life's journey.

Introduction

Aging is an inevitable part of life, and as we journey through the later years, we accumulate a wealth of wisdom and experiences. These valuable insights can be a source of inspiration and guidance for future generations. By sharing our legacy and life reflections, we have the opportunity to leave a lasting impact and face the challenges of aging with grace. In this article, we explore the significance of sharing our wisdom, the benefits it brings, and practical ways to do so.

Embracing the Power of Legacy

1. Defining Legacy: Legacy refers to the intangible inheritance we leave behind, encompassing our values, beliefs, lessons learned, and experiences.

2. Leaving a Lasting Impact: Sharing our legacy helps to preserve our values and life lessons for future generations, providing them with guidance and inspiration.

3. Continuity and Connection: Legacy allows us to connect with our past, present, and future selves, creating a sense of continuity and belonging.

Reflecting on Life's Journey

1. Importance of Reflection: Reflecting on our life experiences helps us make sense of our journey, understand ourselves better, and gain perspective on the challenges and triumphs we have faced.

2. Gaining Wisdom: Through reflection, we can distill the lessons we've learned and the wisdom we've gained, providing valuable insights for ourselves and others.

3. Embracing Gratitude: Reflecting on our blessings and expressing gratitude enhances our well-being and nurtures a positive outlook on life.

Sharing Your Wisdom

1. Writing a Memoir: Penning down your life story in the form of a memoir allows you to share your experiences, emotions, and life lessons with others.

2. Recording Oral Histories: Conducting interviews or recording conversations with loved ones can capture their unique stories and preserve their wisdom for future generations.

3. Blogging or Journaling: Utilizing digital platforms or personal journals provides a creative outlet for self-expression and allows for the dissemination of your thoughts and experiences.

4. Joining Support Groups or Workshops: Engaging in support groups or workshops specifically tailored for sharing life experiences can provide a nurturing environment to express yourself and connect with others.

The Benefits of Sharing

1. Inspiring Others: By sharing your wisdom, you have the potential to inspire and motivate others to overcome challenges, find their purpose, and lead fulfilling lives.

2. Strengthening Family Bonds: Sharing your legacy and life reflections fosters deeper connections within your family, promoting understanding, empathy, and a sense of belonging.

3. Leaving a Positive Mark: Leaving a positive impact on future generations helps shape a better world by imparting valuable lessons, promoting empathy, and encouraging personal growth.

Overcoming Challenges

1. Vulnerability and Courage: Sharing personal stories and experiences requires vulnerability and courage. Embrace these qualities as you open up and share your wisdom.

2. Overcoming Technological Barriers: Embrace technology to reach a wider audience. Seek help if needed to navigate digital platforms or recording devices.

3. Honoring Privacy: Be mindful of privacy concerns when sharing personal stories, ensuring that the consent and comfort of those involved are respected.

Conclusion

As we age, it becomes increasingly important to reflect on our life journey, distill our wisdom, and share our experiences with others. By embracing the power of legacy and leaving a lasting impact, we can inspire future generations, strengthen family bonds, and shape a better world. Whether through writing, recording, or engaging in support groups, sharing your legacy and life reflections can be a transformative and fulfilling experience. So, let us face the challenges of aging with grace and embrace the opportunity to leave a legacy of wisdom, love, and resilience.

"Facing the Challenges of Aging with Grace" is an insightful and comprehensive guidebook that offers valuable guidance and practical advice to individuals navigating the complexities of growing older. This book delves into various aspects of aging, presenting a holistic approach to address the physical, mental, emotional, and social dimensions of this life stage. Each chapter offers a wealth of knowledge, ranging from understanding the challenges and opportunities of aging, challenging ageism and discrimination, and promoting inclusivity, to exploring topics such as physical health and wellness, mental health and cognitive functioning, nutrition and healthy eating, exercise and physical activity, managing chronic pain, adapting to age-related vision and hearing loss, and coping with social isolation and loneliness.

Furthermore, it covers important subjects like enhancing relationships, financial planning and retirement, caregiving and long-term care, embracing technology, maintaining independence, coping with loss and grief, nurturing spirituality, finding purpose and meaning in retirement, and reflecting upon one's legacy and life experiences. By providing practical strategies and empowering insights, this book equips readers with the tools necessary to face the challenges of aging with grace, resilience, and a renewed sense of purpose.

ABOUT THE AUTHOR

Mr. C. P. Kumar is a retired Scientist 'G' from National Institute of Hydrology, Roorkee, Uttarakhand, India. He is also a Reiki Healer and Chakra Balancing practitioner (with pendulum dowsing) and offers Emotional Freedom Technique (EFT) to help individuals with emotional issues. Mr. Kumar has authored many books on technical, spiritual, and social topics.

For further details, you may visit his webpage
https://www.angelfire.com/nh/cpkumar/virgo.html

www.ingramcontent.com/pod-product-compliance
Lightning Source LLC
Chambersburg PA
CBHW061354140726
47997CB00003B/1199